T0011669

What Is Stress?

by Mari Schuh

PEBBLE
a capstone imprint

Pebble Explore is published by Pebble, an imprint of Capstone
1710 Roe Crest Drive
North Mankato, Minnesota 56003
www.capstonepub.com

Library of Congress Cataloging-in-Publication Data
Names: Schuh, Mari C., 1975- author.
Title: What is stress? / by Mari Schuh.
Description: North Mankato : Capstone Press, [2021] | Series:
Health and my body | Includes bibliographical references and index.
| Audience: Ages 6-8 | Audience: Grades 2-3 | Summary: "Stress
can make you feel bad. It can be caused by lots of different things.
A big test. A fight with a friend. A new experience. But no matter
what causes the stress, what's important is how you deal with it"—
Provided by publisher.
Identifiers: LCCN 2020032596 (print) | LCCN 2020032597 (ebook)
| ISBN 9781977132222 (hardcover) | ISBN 9781977133243
(paperback) | ISBN 9781977155313 (pdf) | ISBN 9781977156938
(kindle edition)
Subjects: LCSH: Stress (Psychology)—Juvenile literature. | Stress
management—Juvenile literature.
Classification: LCC BF575.S75 S367 2021 (print) | LCC BF575.S75
(ebook) | DDC 155.9/042—dc23
LC record available at https://lccn.loc.gov/2020032596
LC ebook record available at https://lccn.loc.gov/2020032597

Image Credits
iStockphoto: FangXiaNuo, 12; FatCamera, 24; Image Source, 17;
kate_sept2004, 5; Shutterstock: ANURAK PONGPATIMET, 16; Daisy
Daisy, 9; Halfpoint, 25; imtmphoto, 19; Jenn Huls, 14; kryzhov, 15;
michaeljung, 23; Monkey Business Images, 21, 26; Motortion Films, 7;
photonova, design element throughout; pingdao, 8; Rawpixel.com, 13;
Romrodphoto, 22; Suzanne Tucker, 11; T.TATSU, 29; wavebreakmedia,
cover; Zivica Kerkez, 6

Editorial Credits
Editor: Christianne Jones; Designer: Sarah Bennett; Media Researcher:
Morgan Walters; Production Specialist: Laura Manthe

All internet sites appearing in back matter were available and
accurate when this book was sent to press.

Table of Contents

Stressed Out.................................... 4

Signs of Stress 6

What Makes People Stressed?.......... 12

Dealing with Stress 20

Glossary 30

Read More........................ 31

Internet Sites 31

Index 32

Bold words are in the glossary.

Stressed Out

Nate is worried about a test. Riley feels nervous about a sleepover. They are feeling **stress**. It is OK to have stress. Everyone gets stressed.

Think about a time when you were stressed. How did you act? How did you feel? What made you feel that way? What did you do to feel better?

Lots of stress can be bad for you. But some stress can be good. It helps you prepare for things.

Signs of Stress

Stress might last a long time. You could be stressed about taking a test all week. Or it can be over quickly. You might only be stressed about the test right before you take it.

Stress affects people in different ways. Some people get mad. Stress can make people cry. Other people want to be alone.

It's important to know how you feel when you get stressed. Then you can be prepared to handle the stress.

Stress affects your body in different ways. Your heart beats faster. You breathe faster. Your muscles tighten. You could sweat or feel dizzy. You might feel tired. You might **fidget**. You might get a headache.

Some people feel sick and can't eat. Other people eat more food during stressful times. Some people are not hungry at all.

Stress can change how you sleep. Some people sleep more when they are stressed. Others can't fall asleep. Some people have nightmares. Even after a full night of sleep you might feel tired.

Stress also affects how people act and feel. Stress can make people crabby. Some people might yell. Other people might stay quiet. Or your feelings might change quickly. You can feel fine one minute. The next minute you feel scared, sick, or sad.

Maria feels lonely when she is stressed. She gets sad and quiet. Stress makes Ben tired. He doesn't have energy. He doesn't feel like playing sports.

What Makes People Stressed?

What causes stress? So many things! Losing a library book can cause stress. Fighting with your brother might make you upset. Going to the doctor can be stressful.

Being **bullied** or teased makes people stressed. They feel nervous and sad. Being rushed can cause stress. People feel like they do not have enough time. They might hurry. Then they might make mistakes.

Things that make you worry cause stress. Lydia's dog needs surgery. She has been worried all week. Lydia can't eat or sleep. Oliver's grandpa is sick. He is worried. Oliver has a hard time doing his homework or **focusing** in school.

Things that make you scared can cause stress. Sal is scared of big dogs. He gets stressed when his neighbor's dog barks at him. Cami watched a scary movie before bed. Her heart was racing. Now Cami can't sleep.

Big life changes often cause stress. It takes time to get used to new things. Give yourself time to adjust.

Jada's mom had a baby. Now Jada is a big sister. Everyone is focused on the baby. Jada feels left out. This makes her feel stressed.

Ezra started a new school. He feels lonely. He is worried about making new friends and fitting in.

Sometimes your family might make you feel stressed. Your mom and dad are fighting. Maybe your mom is traveling a lot for work. Maybe your brother is being mean to you.

When you are stressed, it's important to talk about it. Tell adults you trust. Talk about how you feel. Adults can find ways to help you feel **calmer**. Sometimes, just talking helps get rid of stress! Writing in a journal can make you feel better too.

Dealing with Stress

There are many things you can do to have less stress. Everyone is different. What helps one person might not be great for you. Try different things. See what works best for you.

Some kids might get stressed when they are too busy. They might need more free time. Then they can rest and play when they want. They might like alone time as well.

Other kids enjoy having the same **schedule** every day. They like having a **routine** and keeping busy. They might like hanging out with friends every day and don't need as much alone time.

Taking good care of yourself can help lower your stress. Get plenty of sleep. When people are tired, they often feel more stressed. Try to go to bed at the same time each night.

Eat healthy foods like vegetables and fruits. Drink lots of water. You will have more energy and feel great!

Having fun can help stress go away. Smile and laugh! Dance around your room. Tell a joke. Do things you enjoy. Maybe you like playing music or making art. Or maybe you like to read or write.

Watch your favorite movie. Play with a pet. Go fishing. Hug your mom or dad. Play catch with a friend. Go for a hike. Or sit and do nothing. Soon, you will feel better.

Being active helps you get rid of stress. Be sure to move your body. Play outside. Go to the park with friends. Take a walk. Go for a bike ride. Limit your time on phones and computers.

You can relax your body when you are feeling stressed. Close your eyes. Take deep, slow breaths. Feel the air go in and out. Stretch your body. Do **yoga**. Then you will feel calm.

Stress is a part of life. It is OK to be stressed sometimes. In fact, it's important to feel stress. But what's more important is finding healthy ways to deal with it. You know how stress affects you. So only you know how to make yourself feel better.

Relax and rest. Be active and play. Take good care of yourself. Ask for help. Learn from stressful times. Then you will be happy and healthy!

Glossary

bully (BUL-ee)—to be mean, to scare, or pick on someone

calm (KAHM)—quiet and peaceful

fidget (FIJ-it)—to keep moving because you are nervous, bored, or restless

focus (FOH-kuss)—to keep all your attention

routine (roo-TEEN)—a set of tasks done in a set order

schedule (SKEJ-ul)—a plan telling when things will happen

stress (STRESS)—worry, strain, or pressure

yoga (YOH-guh)—exercises and ways of breathing that keep the mind and body healthy

Read More

Collins, Jordan. *It's Great to Keep Calm.* New York: Children's Press, 2020.

Kawa, Katie. *What Happens When Someone Has Anxiety?* New York: KidHaven Publishing, 2019.

Loh-Hagan, Virginia. *Chill Out: Practicing Calm.* Ann Arbor, MI: Cherry Lake Publishing, 2020.

Internet Sites

KidsHealth: Stress
kidshealth.org/en/kids/stress.html

KidsHealth: Worry Less in 3 Steps
kidshealth.org/en/kids/worry-less.html?WT.ac=p-ra

PBS Kids: Draw Your Feelings
pbskids.org/arthur/health/resilience/draw-your-feelings.html

Index

being active, 27, 28
body reactions, 8, 9, 15

crying, 7

dancing, 24

eating, 9, 14, 23

family, 18
feeling
  bullied, 13
  calm, 18, 27
  crabby, 10
  happy, 28
  left out, 16
  lonely, 17
  mad, 7
  nervous, 4, 13
  quiet, 10, 11
  rushed, 13
  sad, 10, 11, 13
  scared, 10, 15
  sick, 10
  teased, 13
  tired, 11, 22
  upset, 12
  worried, 4, 14

fighting, 12
friends, 17, 21, 27

having fun, 24

playing, 20, 24, 25, 27, 28

reading, 24
relaxing, 27, 28

sleeping, 10, 14, 15, 22
spending time alone, 7, 20, 21
stretching, 27

talking, 18

writing, 18, 24